D0936305

3-10-04   X

Author:
Andrew Langley is the author of a large number of non-fiction books for both children and adults, many of them on historical subjects. He lives in Bath, England.

Artist:
David Antram was born in Brighton, England, in 1958. He studied at Eastbourne College of Art and then worked in advertising for 15 years before becoming a full-time artist. He has illustrated many children's non-fiction books.

Series Creator:
David Salariya was born in Dundee, Scotland. He has illustrated a wide range of books and has created and designed many new series for publishers both in the U.K. and overseas. In 1989 he established The Salariya Book Company. He lives in Brighton with his wife, the illustrator Shirley Willis, and their son Jonathan.

Editor:
Karen Barker Smith

Editorial Assistant:
Stephanie Cole

Created, designed and produced by
The Salariya Book Company Ltd
25 Marlborough Place,
Brighton BN1 1UB

ISBN 0-531-14599-9 (Lib. Bdg.)
ISBN 0-531-16205-2 (Pbk.)

Published in America by Franklin Watts
Grolier Publishing Co., Inc.
90 Sherman Turnpike, Danbury, CT 06816

Visit Franklin Watts on the internet
at: http://publishing.grolier.com

A CIP catalog record for this title is available from the Library of Congress.

Printed and bound in China

You Wouldn't Want to Be a Viking Explorer!

Chaaaarge!

Voyages You'd Rather Not Make

Written by
Andrew Langley

Illustrated by
David Antram

Created and designed by
David Salariya

W

FRANKLIN WATTS
A Division of Grolier Publishing
NEW YORK • LONDON • HONG KONG • SYDNEY
DANBURY, CONNECTICUT

Contents

Introduction

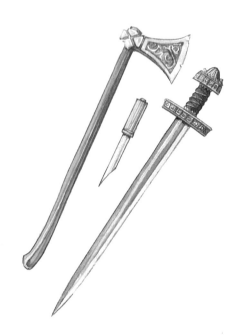

The Viking people originally lived in small communities in Scandinavia in northern Europe, raising crops and livestock, fishing, and trading goods with their neighbors. Each community was ruled by a king or chieftain. By about A.D. 790 the population had grown too large, so the Vikings began to explore other lands in search of territory and booty. Raiders crossed the sea to attack England, Ireland, and Scotland. With their swift long ships and bloodthirsty ways, they terrified coastal villages and seized large areas of land.

By the 850s, the Vikings of Sweden and Norway had established powerful trading towns in northern Europe. Norwegian settlers began to colonize Iceland, where the climate was much like their homeland's, and a century later, a Viking called Erik the Red reached Greenland and set up a new colony. In the 10th century, Leif Ericsson was the first Viking to cross the unknown ocean to the west and venture to North America.

As an adventurous young Viking, you are eager to join another group of explorers who plan to follow in Leif's footsteps in search of a new life elsewhere. You will travel vast distances across the Atlantic Ocean in a long ship, to the coast of a new continent. It will be a difficult and dangerous journey — you really wouldn't want to be a Viking explorer!

Greenland: Looking for a Way Out

Vikings first discovered Greenland about A.D. 982. Their leader, Erik the Red, thought it was a fine place for a settlement, so he sailed back to Iceland and told his people. Erik called it "green land" to make them think there was rich soil for farming as well as caribou and fish for food and bears and foxes to hunt for their furs. Hundreds of Vikings followed him to the new country and you were one of them. But what a disappointment! The land is not very green at all — it is cold and few crops grow. How can you escape to find a better life?

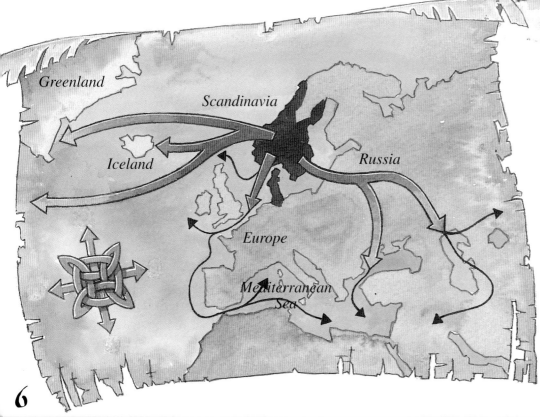

Greenland

Scandinavia

Iceland

Russia

Europe

Mediterranean Sea

The Viking World

The Vikings spread out from Scandinavia in search of new land and freedom from their harsh rulers. Some went across Europe, reaching Russia and the Mediterranean. Others traveled west to what is now known as Iceland, Greenland, and North America.

My name is Radnor Lothbrok (hairy trousers). My life is dull, dull, dull...

Handy Hint

Nasty smell!

Try to avoid living near your town's workshop, where they make leather from animal skins. The stink is disgusting!

Choose me!

SAILORS WANTED. Thorvald, Leif Ericsson's brother, is planning an expedition! He is going to explore another new land across the sea to the west, and wants brave men to row his ship. You volunteer at once, eager for some adventure.

The Long Ship

Members of the crew load the ship with food, water, and other supplies for the voyage. The ship is long and narrow, made from oak planks that curve upward at each end. The planks are fitted together with iron nails, and any gaps are plugged with tar and animal hair. The ship is very shallow — the distance from the bottom to the gunwale is only about 6 ft (1.8 m). Along each side are 16 holes for the oars to slide through. The holes can be shut in rough weather to keep out the sea.

What Will You Take With You?

There is not much room on board. Most of the cargo has to be stored in the narrow space under the deck. You are taking weapons and tools, as well as casks of water. The hens and goats traveling with you will supply fresh eggs and milk.

Shield

Clothes

Axe

Drinking horn

Sack of grain *Cooking pot*

8

Handy Hint

In rough seas, the boat will need bailing out with buckets. You don't want to sink!

Come on Bjorn! I don't know where we're going either!

OFF YOU GO. You sit down on your sea chest and grip your oar. The helmsman stands at the stern, and Thorvald, the chieftain, stands at the bow. He gives an order and all 32 of you pull on the oars. The adventure has begun!

Sailing Away

Life at Sea

TAKING A BREAK. Once the sail is up, the wind drives the ship along. You can put away your oar and relax. There is no shelter on deck, but you soon get used to the cold.

EATING. In good weather you can go ashore at night and light a fire for cooking. In bad weather the ship stays at sea and you have to chew on cold dried fish.

SLEEPING. To keep warm at night, you snuggle inside a skin sack called a hudfat, normally used for storing tools. But you have to share it with someone else!

Each member of the crew pulls hard on their oars. The long ship moves away from the shore, and a wind springs up. Thorvald orders you to stop rowing and raise the mast. This is made from a tall pine tree trunk, which the crew members place in a slot in the middle of the ship and haul upright. Then they hoist the heavy woolen cloth sail. It soon fills with wind and the ship gathers speed. The helmsman steers with a special oar attached to the stern, keeping the coast on the starboard (right-hand) side.

Come on Short Erik! Push!

Into the Unknown

On the second day, the ship sails further from land. Soon you are in the open sea and will depend on the skills of the helmsman and the chieftain to take you in the right direction. This is a difficult job, for rain is pelting down and the wind whips up the waves. The freezing rain has soaked through your leather clothing and there is not a dry place to sit. Slabs of ice drift past the ship, showing that the Arctic pack ice is not far away to the north. The sail is lowered to prevent it being split by the howling gales and Thorvald orders everyone to get their oars ready. Rowing makes it easier for the helmsman to steer and avoid the dangerous ice floes.

SEASICKNESS. The swell of the sea makes you feel sick, headachy and sleepy. But after a couple of days you get used to the motion of the ship and feel better.

STEERING BY THE STARS. By night, the helmsman can find his course by looking for the Pole Star, always exactly North in the night sky. By day, he steers by the position of the sun.

BRAVE EXPLORERS. From Scandinavia Vikings sailed the unknown to reach the Faeroe Islands, Iceland, and then Greenland. In AD 992, Vikings became the first Europeans to land in what is now known as North America.

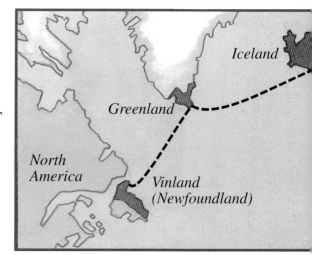

12

Lost! Drifting in a Fog

Once the wind has died down, a thick mist swirls around the ship and chills you to the bone in your soaking wet clothes. The only thing that keeps you warm is the effort of rowing. Worse still, you cannot see anything — the ice floes on the sea and the sun in the sky have disappeared behind the fog. Which course should the helmsman steer? You need to ask for help from the gods. The Viking religion is part of your daily life, with no special priests or temples. Thorvald is the chieftain, so he prays to Odin, the father of all the gods, and to Thor, the god of the sky and ruler of storms.

We're lost!

Finding the Way

It is easy to navigate when you can see the coast. You simply follow a series of known landmarks. In open sea, it is more difficult. Avoiding icebergs and pack ice can easily send you off course.

HERE COMES THE SUN.
The gods answer the prayers and the sun breaks through the clouds. The helmsman can now work out the course westwards – the direction taken by the two expeditions which have made the voyage before.

Steam
Steam
Steam

Handy Hint

Slop

Every few days, rub the fat from sheep or other animals into your goatskin boots. This will keep them soft and waterproof.

We're not lost. We just don't know where we are.

Land at Last!

The next morning you are awoken by a shout, "Land ahead!" You can see from the long ship that the coast of this mysterious new land is mountainous and icy, with no grass or trees. Thorvald recognizes this as Helluland, or "flat rock land," the place Leif Ericsson had described after his own voyage. The helmsman turns the ship to follow the coast southward, and the landscape becomes more promising.

FINDING LAND. Thorvald followed the route taken by his brother Leif, heading west across the sea until he saw land.

BEACHING THE BOAT. The crew must leap ashore and grab ropes to haul the ship as far up the beach as they can. This will stop it from being washed away.

LEIF ERICSSON, son of Erik the Red, sailed west about A.D. 1000 in search of new land and timber supplies.

Now, according to Leif, this must be Vinland.

Leif landed on the coast of North America (probably Newfoundland).

16

You reach what Leif called Markland, or "wood land," which is flat and thickly covered with forests. Finally, you arrive at Vinland, or "wine land," where the climate is warmer. Thorvald leads his crew ashore. But what dangers are lurking?

Handy Hint

Use tree trunks as rollers to haul your ship over land. This means you can bypass any waterfalls and rapids that would stop your progress up a river.

Grrrr

Turf and Timber: Building a Settlement

Making Wine:

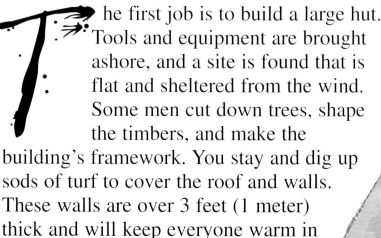

GATHERING THE BERRIES. Huge red huckleberries grow here. You can turn them into wine.

The first job is to build a large hut. Tools and equipment are brought ashore, and a site is found that is flat and sheltered from the wind. Some men cut down trees, shape the timbers, and make the building's framework. You stay and dig up sods of turf to cover the roof and walls. These walls are over 3 feet (1 meter) thick and will keep everyone warm in winter when a fire is burning in the stone hearth.

Squash

CRUSHING. Put the berries in a bucket and squash them with a piece of wood. Leave the juice to ferment into wine.

DRINKING. Making wine is a good way to preserve the juice of wild fruits. You can drink the wine through the cold winter.

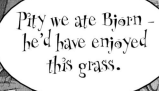

Pity we ate Bjorn – he'd have enjoyed this grass.

Hundreds of seabirds have nests on the coast's cliffs. Steal their eggs to make a quick meal.

Handy Hint

FISHING. The sea is full of fish such as cod and herring, and there are salmon and eels in the rivers. All these can be dried and salted to preserve them for winter.

Winter in Vinland

I n Greenland, the winters are long and extremely cold, with short days and many hours of darkness. But Vinland is a lot further south, so summer here is much longer and winter not so cold. There is less snow, and grass continues to grow for most of the year. All the same, you have to spend many winter evenings huddled around the smoky fire in your hut. You pass the time by telling each other tales about the great deeds of ancient heroes and gods, such as the terrifying Thor and his mighty hammer, Mjollnir.

EXPLORING INLAND. In summer, Thorvald leads an expedition into the mountains and forests to the west. You find the lakes rich with fish and the woods full of animals such as bears, deer and antelopes.

BOARD GAMES. You all like to play hnefatafl (say 'nefatal'), a game like chess, where you move pieces to try and capture the king.

Valkyrie

Thor

CARVING. Many Vikings are skilled at carving objects from wood or bone. They make figures of gods, or everyday items like spoons and bowls.

Frey

You're Not Alone! The Skraelings

The First Americans

Thousands of years ago, an ice cap joined the continents of Asia and North America.

One day, you find three rocks on the seashore, but they seem to be made of wood or leather. You and your companions tip them over, and there, huddled underneath, are some people! You had no idea anybody else lived in this remote place. The strangers jump up in panic, terrified at the sight of your weapons.

The first American peoples probably walked over the ice from Asia into North America about 20,000 years ago. From here, they slowly spread out and made settlements. The Vikings called them "skraelings."

The skraelings were hiding under their boats, made of seal or moose skins stretched over wooden frames.

And don't pretend to be rocks again!

The Vikings are hostile to anyone who is not one of them and kill some of the strangers. Those who escape go back to their people, so the skraclings, or "screaming barbarians," could now be planning a revenge attack. These skraelings were probably hunters who traveled south in search of seals and seabirds.

Handy Hint

Always keep your sword sharp — you never know when you might need it!

AAaaah!

AAaaah!

Hunting and Storing Food

Shield

Helmet

During the autumn, you must gather and store enough food to last through the winter. There is wild wheat growing on the seashore, and nuts and berries in the forest. There are plenty of animals to hunt for meat. The largest and most valuable prey are whales, which give a huge supply of meat as well as oil, skin, and bones. But whale hunts are perilous. You must row out in a small boat and get as near the whale as you can. One man hurls a harpoon. It sticks into the whale, which then tries to escape, dragging you along behind. Only when the whale becomes tired can you kill it with spears.

Splash

Splash

STORING FOOD. Fish and meat are preserved by hanging them to dry in the wind, or by "pickling" in salty water. Even pine bark was stored, to eat if everything else ran out!

BLACKSMITH AT WORK. Skilled Viking blacksmiths could make anything from axe-heads to cooking pots. Using tongs to hold hot metal on the anvil, they cut and hammered it into shape.

Weapons

Bow and arrows

Spear

Axe

Dagger

Sword

Vikings are always ready for a fight and carry their weapons with them at all times. They protect their bodies with wooden shields and iron helmets. They fight with long-handled axes, double-edged swords, iron-tipped arrows, and spears for throwing and jabbing. When they run into battle, they sometimes howl like wolves to terrify the enemy.

Handy Hint

Deep freeze your meat by packing it in ice and snow. This will stop it from rotting.

Under Attack!
You and Your Enemy:

By the end of winter, you are all weak and very hungry. The food stores have been used up, and many of your companions have gotten sick. Everyone is feeling homesick for Greenland. You even hope to meet another band of skraelings. Perhaps they will have food to trade in exchange for metal tools or cloth.

Axes and swords with iron blades

GOING BERSERK. Viking warriors sometimes put on a "ber-serk," or bearskin shirt, before going into battle, to help them fight ferociously. This is where we get the phrase "going berserk."

HUNTER-GATHERERS. The skraelings are not such skilled fighters as the Vikings. They aren't obsessed with conquering land so spend most of their time hunting and gathering food.

Flint-tipped arrows and spears

The skraelings return, but they are not here to trade. They want revenge against those who attacked and killed their friends. They rush at you, shooting arrows and throwing spears. The iron weapons of the Vikings drive them off, but someone is hurt. Your chieftain lies fatally wounded by an arrow.

Handy Hint

Women's long hair makes a perfect string for your bow. Pluck a few from a friend's scalp before your journey!

Whoosh!

Whack!

And don't call us skraelings!

27

Going Home

LONG SHIP FUNERAL.
Back at home, Thorvald's funeral would have been much grander. A Viking chief might be buried, or occasionally burned, inside a long ship that would carry him to the next world. With him went all he needed in the next life, including weapons, treasure, clothing, and even horses.

Things are looking very bleak. The skraelings have retreated for the moment, but they'll be back. Chieftain Thorvald is dead and many of your companions are wounded or ill. There is very little food available. The explorers have no choice but to sail away, back to Greenland. You load up the ship with tools and weapons and roll it down to the water's edge, ready for a quick getaway.

Harald →

Alas, poor Thorvald. I knew him well, Harald.

FUNERAL PYRE.
This is only a simple funeral. Animal hides are placed on the pyre with the body on top. The person's belongings, such as his weapons and drinking horn, are placed beside him.

Before you leave, there is a solemn task to perform. You pile up firewood on the beach and put Thorvald's body on top, surrounded by his belongings. Then you set fire to the funeral pyre. As you row away and begin the cold and dangerous journey home, you watch the flames roaring up into the sky.

Handy Hint

Carve a message to mark your visit before you leave. Use a rune stick inscribed with the symbols of the runic alphabet as a guide.

And don't come back!

Oh well, back to a dull, dull life. I can't wait!

Glossary

Anvil A heavy iron block with a flat top used as a surface on which to beat hot metal.

Bail out To scoop out water from inside a boat.

Booty Goods taken by force or won in a war.

Bow The front end of a boat or ship.

Caribou North American deer, much like reindeer.

Colony A group of settlers in a new country who are still ruled by their country of origin.

Ferment The chemical change that makes fruit juice into an alcoholic drink.

Frey The Viking god of fertility, who was responsible for crops growing well.

Funeral pyre A platform of firewood on which a dead body is laid and burned.

Gunwale The upper edge of the side of a boat or ship.

Harpoon A spearlike weapon attached to a long rope, used for catching whales.

Helluland The Viking name for what is now known as Baffin Island, Canada.

Helmsman The member of a ship's crew who steers the ship.

Hnefatafl A Viking board game similar to chess; it means "king's table."

Hudfat A bag made from animal skins and used for storing equipment.

Ice floe A piece of flat, floating ice.

Markland The Viking name for the area probably on the coast of Labrador, Canada.

Mediterranean Sea The sea that lies between Europe and North Africa.

North Star A star in the Little Bear constellation that shows the direction of due North.

Odin The Viking god of battle and king of the gods.

Pack ice An area of sea crowded with large pieces of floating ice.

Runes The letters of an alphabet used by Vikings and other Norse peoples.

Scandinavia The region of northern Europe made up of Iceland, Norway, Sweden, and Denmark.

Sea chest A strong wooden box in which sailors used to store their belongings.

Stern The back end of a boat or ship.

Thor The Viking god of thunder and son of Odin.

Valkyrie Female warriors who were daughters of the god Odin. They carried dead heroes from the battlefield to Valhalla, the castle of the afterlife.

Viking The word means piracy or raiding.

Index